The Undoing

Elizabeth Stott

Maytree Press 2023

Published 2023 by Maytree Press

www.maytreepress.co.uk

ISBN: 978-1-913508-33-6

A CIP catalogue record of this book is available from the British Library.

Cover image: Spooky Action at a Distance

© Alison Critchlow

Maytree 042

Acknowledgements

In the Shape of Men, I Have Your Words and *Afterlight* appeared in Porridge Magazine. *Ladybird* was published in Under the Radar. *Save Me* took second place in a Magma Magazine subscribers' competition. *Candidate* appeared in The Writers' Café Magazine. *Reconstruction* was included in the Write to be Counted Anthology. *Knowing* was published in The Butchers' Dog Magazine, and *I Grow My Hair* in Mslexia. *The Phenomenon* appeared in SpeakEasy Magazine.

About the Author

Elizabeth Stott writes poetry and fiction, particularly short stories. She was born in Kent, and has moved north in stages, settling in Cumbria where she has lived for over 25 years. A physics graduate, she worked in industry before taking time out to raise her family. As an antidote to the domestic, she started writing fiction and poetry, which has developed to include work in varied form and genre. She has published work in magazines, anthologies, for spoken word events, as a Nightjar Press chapbook and a collection of fiction, *Familiar Possessions.*

Dedicated to my husband and children, with love.

And in memory of my brother, John.

Contents:

In the Shape of Men

We made the heads of Styrofoam
so not to be too heavy on their frail necks.
Hearts? Simply-fashioned, from lumps of stone.

Arms, legs - bent sticks.
Torsos were fabricated from chicken wire and some kind
of pliable fabric. Enough to hold

it all together. Give them a plausible
sense of form. We didn't make them too clever,
after what happened last time.

Ladybird

Wait
for him
an afternoon.

Watch
the slow march
of light across the room.
Watch a blank-faced door.
Wait.
Read the pamphlet given.

A tea tray rattles.

Glimpse
a polished desk
a row of family portraits in wooden frames:
perhaps – a wife, children.
Read the pamphlet given.

Maybe
you'll notice the blue carpet,
a scattering of biscuit crumbs
a place where the pile is worn.
Read the pamphlet given.

See the little ladybird trapped by the glass.
It wants to go home. It wants to go home.

Save Me

I find I am tied to a past over which I had limited influence.
Open the past. Open my past.
Can confirm birthdate, attendance at a mixed infant's school from
<insert date>
where I learned to write numerals on a slate,
with chalk, as we all did in those days. No paper.
Later, I mastered decimal and other forms of numerical notation
at schools far from that place.
But you don't need to know about that.   Cough.
The computer remembers for me. I can't wipe the numbers away
with a cloth.
But my fingerprint is a persistent nuisance requiring alcohol wipes.
But can write what the heck I like and delete
/deleted it. Ha! Click Save. Not, Send,
*for ****'s sake.*

I can see you expect me to be open about memories.
Perhaps I don't trust you too much. I know something of algorithms.
(Algorithm is an anagram of logarithm.)
My name is not as it says on the tin: *invisible typing.*
My first car was a <Hillman >.
Its bodywork was aluminium.
No seatbelts. Squeaky brakes. But you don't care about the danger.
And those seats were hard.
Hardly anyone knows
that it was <blue>. (Kind of.) But I just told you. (Kind of me.)
You want the date of my marriage? <insert date>.
The town of my birth?
<insert name> The street where I grew up? <insert whatever>.
Where did I meet my husband? <forget it>
What is my favourite food?   The name of my childhood pet... ?
They are on different mind maps. Guess me if you can.
There is a chance I'll forget these things. Save me just in lower case.
Open the future.
Save me on some benighted server.
Just in case.

Your Zoom Mother

I am your Zoom mother
I love you no less
than the one you know at home.

I dress more smartly than she does
because I need you to think
that your real mum is keeping her shit together

and not letting herself go.
Although, Zoom can't do anything
about my hair. Blame the software.

But your Zoom mother, darling,
loves you every bit as much
as your real mother

who is also struggling with her hair.
Blame lockdown. No hairdressers.
She made a cake for your birthday.

I light the candles for you to see
and make a bad joke about freezing the cake
candles and all. But the flames

wouldn't freeze well. Ha ha. I must
let you know that your real mother promises
to make you a real cake sometime soon.

Candidate

The woman is annoyed because
the rain makes her hair frizz.
She worries that the cloud around her head
makes her seem nebulous. Unfocussed.
But she wants this job, she really does.

In her new business suit
she walks the street
in tight, shiny shoes,
until she comes to a big door marked 'push'.
And she pushes it, hard. And

the door opens wide.
Everything is as impressive as she imagined;
a gleaming glass atrium, rising to the sun. On reception
there's a smart and smiling young woman,
confident in her tailored dress. Corporate logo
embroidered on her breast, like an owner's label.

I'm here for an interview…

The girl's smile sets.
There's a dash of condescension in the manicured voice.
Let me take your name.
I'll check the list…

The girl's hair is slicked tight, slapped into place,
make-up too perfect for mistakes.
The woman can feel her hair spring out,
freed from product and spray.
It seems to rise like thistledown,
hovers in a cloud around her face.
Who can own her with a halo like this?

Reconstruction

My friend wishes to re-make herself from sackcloth and ashes.

Take the ashes of stars, I advise,
and sackcloth made
from the recycled garments of saints.

You don't live with the scars, she replies.

Months later, after doing nothing,
she decides on brown paper and string.

I tell her that she must use brown paper shaved
from the sunlight that skims fields of ripe grain at harvest –
string twisted from the hair of mermaids.

She tells me I should reconsider the blonde streaks, go on a diet.

For a year, her clothes make her look like a parcel,
covering her from shoulder to knee.

I am so lucky, I know. I carry on with my sympathy,
stop wearing low-cut blouses in her company.

Abruptly, she moves on.
Her wrapping is gone, leaving a soft, pale form.
She says that sand and straw will do to pad her out.

Then take the sand from eternity's hourglass I tell her,
and the straw from the stable of a unicorn.

Apparently, I am fatuous, and possibly insane.
I go away – reconsider the blonde streaks, go on a diet.

In my absence, she fashions for herself a golden bodice,
more beautiful than the breastplate of a queen's battledress.

Knowing

She slips the loose dress right off
when the young doctor comes to examine her.
She wears nothing underneath
and the doctor can see everything.
Coyly, she looks up at him,
knowing he can see her body
with the eyes of a man.

He asks the nurse to help her to dress.
But not before he sees the sores,
the flaps where breasts once swelled,
the pubis bare and purpled, the sagging skin
that seems to have no connection with the bones
that try to shape a woman's lovely frame
out of the past tense.

Later, he tells his young wife
that she is beautiful,
that he will always love her.

The Undoing

The girl wears a red dress that has
the texture of coiled wire.
It has a colour between
crushed strawberry
and papaya.

Her eyes say, *beware...*
as she holds out her hand.

I see the lines carved
for life, head, and heart,
and a line for fate
that runs through her palm
like a knife cut.
That's love for you boy…
Her laugh is like a bark.

She spins for me to admire.
Her teeth are sharp.
I see how she is caged in that dress,
how the red thread loops and knots.

It's just one strand, I know.

One tug and it will spring apart.

Festival Dress

That trashy kaftan your gran wears in Tesco
embarrasses you.

But in 69, she wore a mini-skirt,
went dancing, her legs lithe and long.
Then later, in a field, she wore a maxi
splashed with daisies,
and mud.
Night starry with stars,
and sparkling with cider
a man did more than just kiss her…
Your granddad.

Your mum missed out on the maxi.
She danced at the school disco in a silver top.
Oh, oh, electro-
pop.

Your chagrin when your mum went retro
and bought the same festival dress on eBay
you coveted for Glasto…
Let her hair hang long.

You don't know what your mum missed out on.
Ask your gran,
in her trashy kaftan…

I Grow My Hair

I grow my hair until it is wide spread
Of eagle wings. And you run afraid, as a rabbit runs
before the dark shape on the ground.
You raise a small cloud of dust.
I raise you to the sun.

I grow my hair until it is a wide sweep
of ocean. You sail my storms in fear, steer
by the stars and sun until I suck your ship
into my deep currents. Our atoms become one.
We are rain, grass, rabbits.

I grow my hair until it is a wide curl
of light from a supernova. It envelops planets,
tangles the universe. I drag you, screaming, to
oblivion, yet you are made from the dust of stars.
You dream of them.

I grow my hair until it is a wide lick
of a tongue that speaks things men fear more than death.
If you would escape this, then run, my darling, run.
You raise a small cloud of dust.
I raise you to the sun.

Unbreath

You are the atoms you lay claim to right now.
Some you borrow in a moment's breath.
Others stay on short-term tenancies.

They are the ink that writes your story.
But your atoms are not loyal.
They move on.

You are graffiti on the wall of the universe.
Maybe a slogan, or a slander. A doodle.
A back of the envelope calculation

in the smallest of figures.
There is nothing to separate you from the future.
You are it. Breathe out.

The Slip

To be, or not to be.

It wasn't in the script as a question.

There was no script.

There was no mind.

No space.

No time.

There could be no question.

No hot.

No cold.

No light, nor dark.

There was no

dimension.

No

number.

No

dream.

No idea could form in the not-ness.

There was no sound

no

whisper

no

scream.

No thing
to be
or not.

Only,

the play's the thing.

An audience waits behind the curtain…

A cough

a whisper

a wave

an oscillation.

Off-stage:

a prompt:

To be!

Time

is unlocked.

You heard!

Lights!

The stage is set.

Sound!

The script is written…

A measure. A plot.
A slip. A whip, a scorn.
A foot in the door.
A dream of living.

Now you’ve done it.

To be or not is not in question.
It’s the script.
The action.

The play begins…

with a burp.

Something covers its mouth.

Hisses.

Sketches

In the post, we get…

…brochures for comfortable footwear – soft flat shoes for
shopping, sandals for sunshine cruises, grippy-soled boots
for icy winters, slippers with easy fastenings.

Then come the fat catalogues for wine – bottles, boxes, magnums.
Those refined Malbecs – a spicy Gewürztraminer.
Champagne for optimism.

Soft Merlots for evenings that cool all too soon.

Second-hand Jewellery Shop: Customer Notice

The wedding rings here are the property of dead women.

Polished on the inside, like mother-of-pearl. Scratched on the out, like workman's tools.

A thick band for a rich man's wife. A thin one worn down on a poor man's trouble and strife. Guaranteed to bind, for better or for worse. Please feel free to bargain with us.

The Cup

The lippy stuck to the cup spoke on

The tea made too weak or too strong, cooled

The afternoon fell away, carelessly

The tray slipped beneath its burden of words

Lovers in Monochrome:

Grace

Playful, that leaning back over the railing;
his mid-life spine not so playful,
but that loving look from her
makes it graceful.

The late-afternoon sunlight
illuminates that glance,
catches his silver hair,
binds them together;
all the hope for their future
mapped out in light and dark.
We know how it turned out.

Love Seat

They are not
book-ends
but
the two halves of the understanding heart.

Her finger points up to Heaven;
his hands are crossed in his lap.
Patiently, he waits for her
to finish
all she needs to say

Posing for Still Life

The cat disdains the handsome poet who poses by the window
and teases her with dangled string.
She has rich striped tortoiseshell fur, like a royal train,
and blatantly ignores him.
The man is striped by shadows from the outside world.
He will be acclaimed for what he writes.
His wife-to-be reads intelligently.
She is beautiful, like Cleopatra.

Cold Feet

Remembering winter mornings when the milk froze
on the doorstep
raising a silver hat to the snow.

A cold blast through the open door,
an icy path with footprints
of the milkman going to and fro.

Lift the heavy bottle in two little hands,
see the dark left-behind circle on the stone,
an iced-cream neck exposed...

Walk to school in too-big wellingtons,
socks roll down to the toes.

There'll be trouble
when you get home.

The Phenomenon

They were on holiday celebrating their Ruby,
and she'd hitched up the hems of his new trousers
with stitches that puckered.
Her own trousers, too, had the hallmarks of her homely alteration.
She was small-boned, fragile, too short for regular sizes.
One could just imagine her struggling,
like a little girl, with the big dressmaking scissors.

He never expected her to be a good needlewoman,
nor she that he'd carry her things for her all these years.
Out on the lake that afternoon, when she shivers,
he gets her wrap from the canvas bag he always carries
for their holiday things – the bag with the camera in it,
the blood pressure pills, a bottle of water
and the binoculars bought a while back, duty-free,
on some cruise ship or other.

As he drapes the wrap over her shoulders,
a boat he's watching splits a flock of swimming birds – half of them
spooling up from the lake like a lifetime of sunrises all at once,
the other half swimming for their lives on the surface,
but hardly moving against the wake.
He just manages a photograph of the phenomenon,
exclaiming – *how absurd, how unexpected…*
She smiles, looking in another direction at a small island,
where a solitary tree grows, bent with the wind.

He hadn't expected her to be a good needlewoman,
nor she that he'd carry her things all that time.
That he'd keep the sewing kit from a small hotel
they stayed in on their honeymoon.
All those tiny bobbins;
the bright threads still wound tight upon them.

The In-Betweens

You emerge from dusty pages
in faded summers. Sand, sea
and swimming pools.
The foreign holidays.

You both dressed the part.
That jazzy shirt, that colourful dress.
Sporty shades!

You are the man at the bar,
the woman at the beach.
Those places you talked about
as if you'd always be found there.

The friendly couple
in that little restaurant off a cobbled side-street.
Always ready to talk, to share a drink.

We can hear you laugh
from another page.

What about the quiet in-betweens?
The pauses for air, for thought…

Perhaps the pleasant aftermath of a long lunch.
The languid bright summer afternoon
that trailed into shaded evening
with someone you loved.

Alumni

The children are ahead, pretending to be adults
walking and talking fast.
We are dressed like old people.
Even our stooped shoulders look real.
As does the grey hair, the varicose veins.
And in the authentic old-ladyish comfortable heels,
I struggle to keep up.

In a realistic looking lecture room,
using pretty coloured-in diagrams,
they present to us the future.
It is a good game for a while.
Afterwards, there are 'canapés'
on paper plates and we are surprised
when they serve us real wine.
But, of course, it is in plastic cups.

Today, we have learned the price of coffee
in the many cafés we already know about.
Although it seems remarkably expensive to us.
They have shown us our favourite haunts;
the union bar, and that quiet little restaurant
on the corner – where we dated a lifetime ago.
Somehow it has become
a bustling Carluccio's.
All of it is ours,
but our tour ends here.

The city looks cleaner than it should;
the air brighter and noisier
as if life was just beginning.

Green Wine and Salt

Remember Lanzarote?
That little restaurant
on the quay,
the cold, green wine
hot, wrinkled potatoes – salty *papas arrugadas*
with spicy *mojo rojo.*

Middle age seemed
impossibly distant
and the wild turning of the planet
went unnoticed
beneath our sandaled feet.

A ship crawled the horizon
and disappeared.
The sea licked the pebbly beach.

Thoughts of children and pensions
floated high up and away
as dull diamonds of salt
fell onto our plates.

Later, on the beach,
we talked about the house we'd buy,
dipped our toes into the sun-warmed sea.

I Have Your Words

The claim that my dad was an extra-terrestrial alien
is kind of hard to
substantiate.

It's ridiculous to claim
my dad was an alien,
when, clearly, I am one of you.
I'm one of us.

I'm one of us.
I'm from round here
like you.
From this estate.
A house
round the corner from here.

I went to the school round here, too.
The rough one, the one that most of us went to.
The one round the corner from here.
I sat next to a boy who picked his nose.
The teacher picked on me.
The class laughed at me. I speak funny.
I have a speech in,
I'm, im? a pediment. Yeah. I'm, an, impediment.
I can substantiate this.
I have your language.

You can't transubstantiate
my words to say my dad was an extra
territorial. An extra-terrestrial alien.
He was born here, like me.
Born on the estate round the corner from here.
Like you.

My dad went to heaven, Mum said.
She says
I am the proof he ever existed. I can
substantiate his existence
with my body.

Men from the council are coming round.
They have a special van with words on it.
They will sanitise the area. Clean away my words.
Then things will be all clean and bright
around the corner from here.

A Face

Who would have thought
that the tiny spot
on the window frame
where the light caught a jewel
when the rain came in

would become a stream
that would leave a stain
on the wall beneath

reminiscent of

a face.

It was nearly Christmas
so you drew round it in blue pencil
gave it eyebrows
and a halo in yellow crayon.

The rain came some more
and the plaster cracked
like a lightning bolt on the wall
so you gave the face a scar
like Frankenstein
in the film.

And when January came
your father put a new window in
and the rain stopped coming in but
the stain remained
and you still thought it a face of some kind
so you drew on spectacles
a moustache and a big cigar.

Your mother was fed up
so papered the wall
in a tasteful Georgian stripe.

You could have thought
you had imagined it all

until

the paper bubbled up
and peeled away
and you saw a crack like a lightning bolt
and a shape

reminiscent of

a face.

Afterlight

A day in autumn,
when you can still believe in warmth.
The big yellow sun
rolls over soft lavender hilltops,
cupped, as if by hands outstretched,
to catch your falling heart.

The days are short,
but they are not yet pinched
into a few cold hours of grey light.
Those coming days of loneliness,
an empty hearth.

What's left is the last of the afternoon
the hourglass emptying
into the earth.

If you don't know where you're looking,
that generous floating orb of sun
could be rising or setting.
You can fool yourself if you want to.

Inspired by the life and paintings of Percy Kelly

Just Saying

Keep the home fires on the range
There ain't no coke without fire
Rome wasn't burned in a day

All that glitters is not what it seems
Fortune favours the gold
Don't wait for the dead man's shoes

Let us pray for all those lost soles
A watched pot never
takes one for the dream

Keep those plums good and cold
Pipe up the banned
A breast is made clean

Least said soonest
attended in spirit

He who hesitates is glossed over

Live in the foment

Pride goes before us all

Read the list of destructions

All's well that ends